Beginning Manuscript Handwriting

Write your first and last names on the lines below.

This book belongs to

Aa

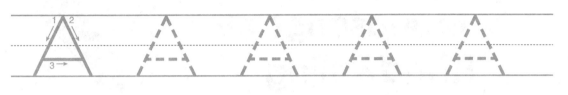

FS109029 • Beginning Manuscript Handwriting

Bb

B B B B B

B B

B B

b b b b b b b b b

b b

FS109029 • Beginning Manuscript Handwriting

Cc

C C C C C

C C

C C

C C C C C C C C

C C

FS109029 • Beginning Manuscript Handwriting

Dd

D D D D D

D D

D D

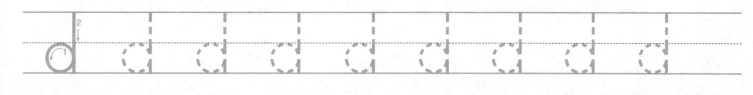

d d d d d d d d d

d d

FS109029 • Beginning Manuscript Handwriting

Ee

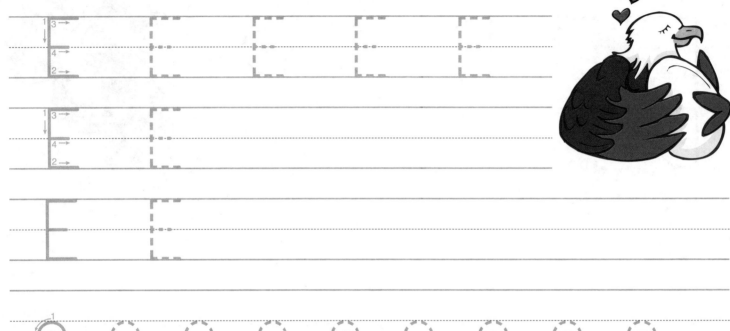

Ff

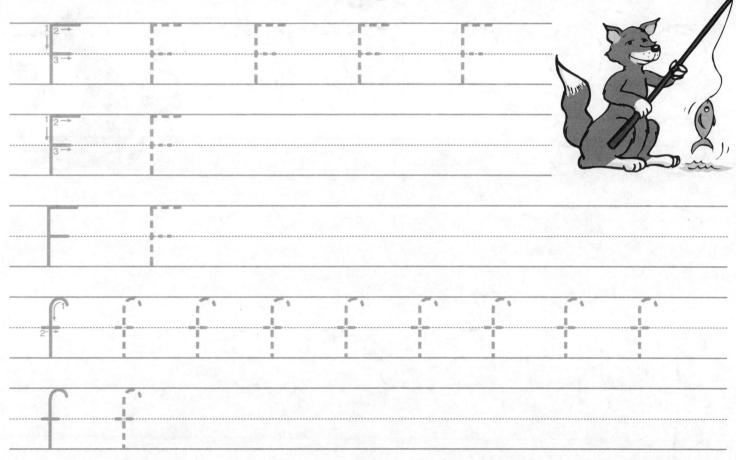

FS109029 • Beginning Manuscript Handwriting

Gg

FS109029 • Beginning Manuscript Handwriting

Hh

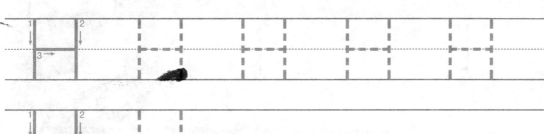

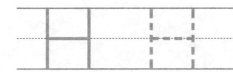

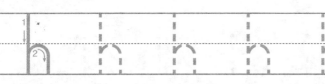

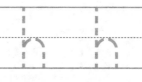

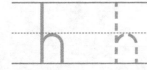

FS109029 • Beginning Manuscript Handwriting

Ii

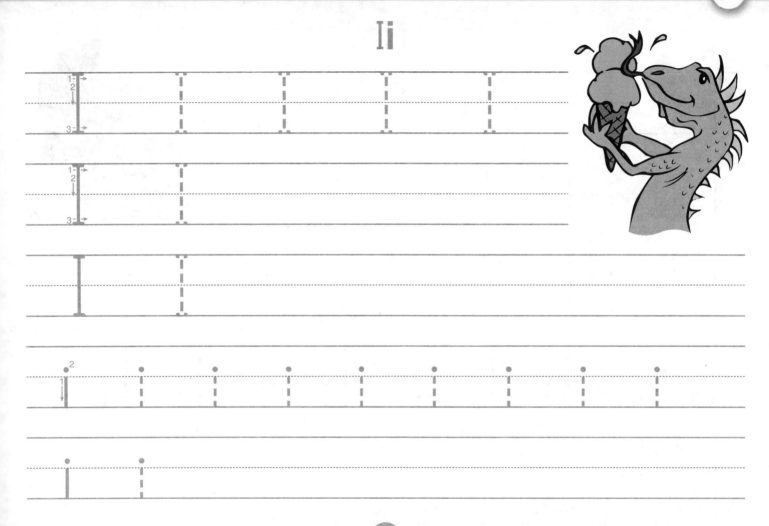

FS109029 • Beginning Manuscript Handwriting

Jj

Kk

© Carson-Dellosa

FS109029 • Beginning Manuscript Handwriting

Ll

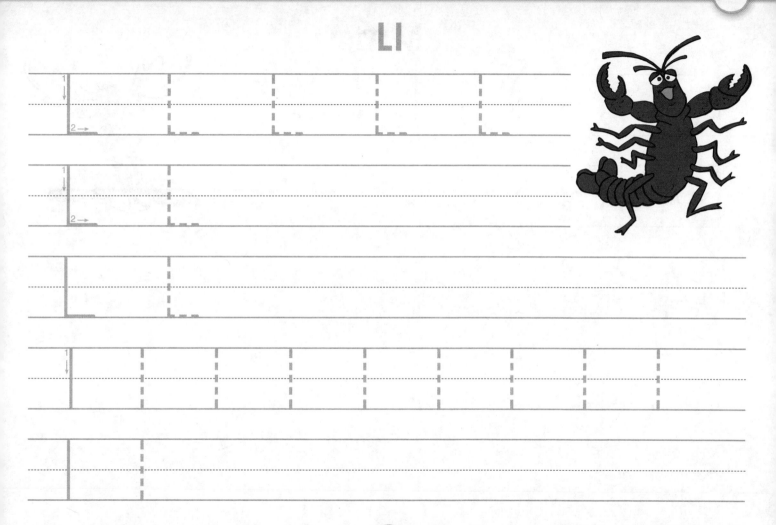

Mm

FS109029 • Beginning Manuscript Handwriting

Nn

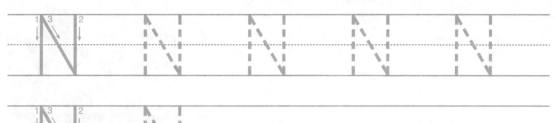

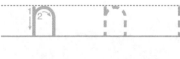

Oo

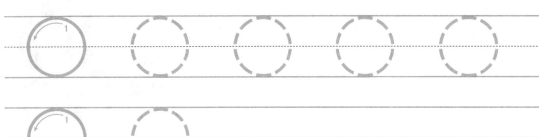

FS109029 • Beginning Manuscript Handwriting

Pp

P P P P P

P P

P P

P P P P P P P P P

P P

FS109029 • Beginning Manuscript Handwriting

Qq

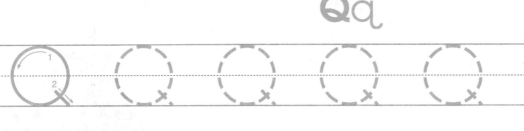

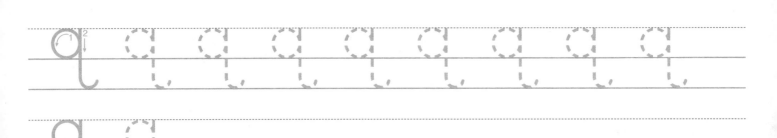

18

FS109029 • Beginning Manuscript Handwriting

Rr

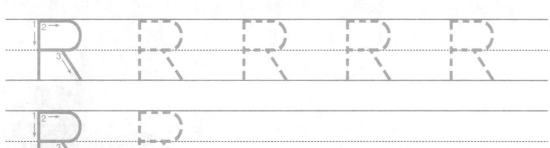

Ss

S S S S S

S S

S S

S S S S S S S S

S S

FS109029 • Beginning Manuscript Handwriting

Tt

Uu

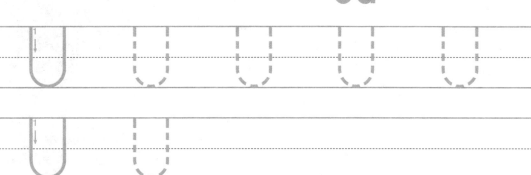

Vv

Ww

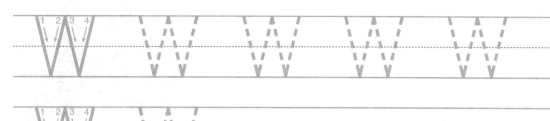

24

FS109029 • Beginning Manuscript Handwriting

Xx

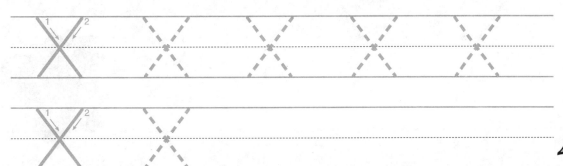

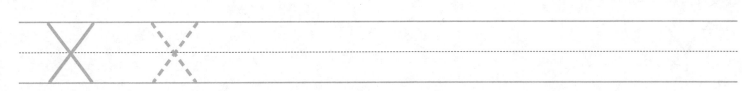

25

FS109029 • Beginning Manuscript Handwriting

Yy

FS109029 • Beginning Manuscript Handwriting

Zz

27

Writing Numbers

FS109029 • Beginning Manuscript Handwriting

Writing Numbers

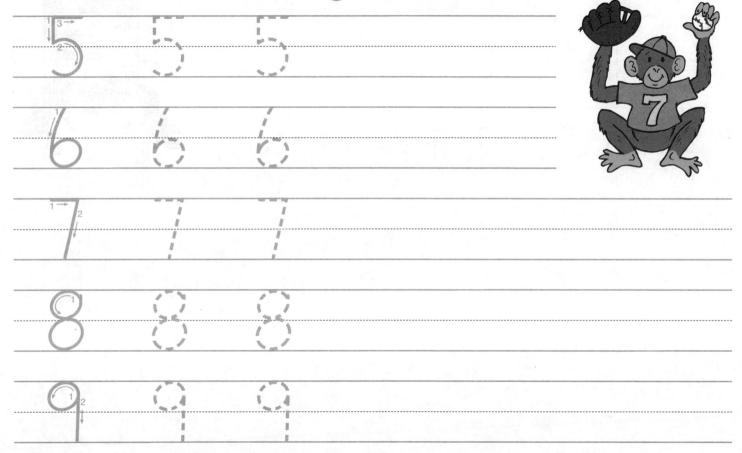

    FS109029 • Beginning Manuscript Handwriting

Aa

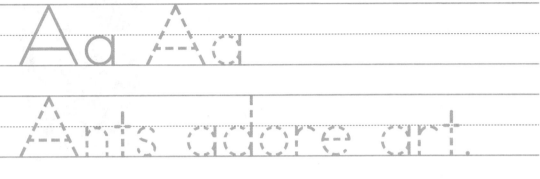

Aa Aa

Ants adore art.

Bb

Bb Bb

Bees buy books.

Cc

Cc Cc

Clowns color cats.

Dd

Dd Dd

Dogs dine on dips.

FS109029 • Beginning Manuscript Handwriting

Ee

Ee Ee

Elves eat eggs.

FS109029 • Beginning Manuscript Handwriting

Ff

Ff Ff

Frogs feed fish.

Gg

Gg Gg

Geese go golfing

FS109029 • Beginning Manuscript Handwriting

Hh

Hh Hh

Horses have hay.

FS109029 • Beginning Manuscript Handwritir

Ii

Ii Ii

Irving Insect is ill.

Jj

Jj Jj

Jays juggle jam.

Kk

Kk Kk

Koalas kiss kittens.

n-Dellosa   FS109029 • Beginning Manuscript Handwriting

Ll

Ll Ll

Lizards lick leaves.

FS109029 • Beginning Manuscript Handwriting

Mm

Mm Mm

Mice make mud.

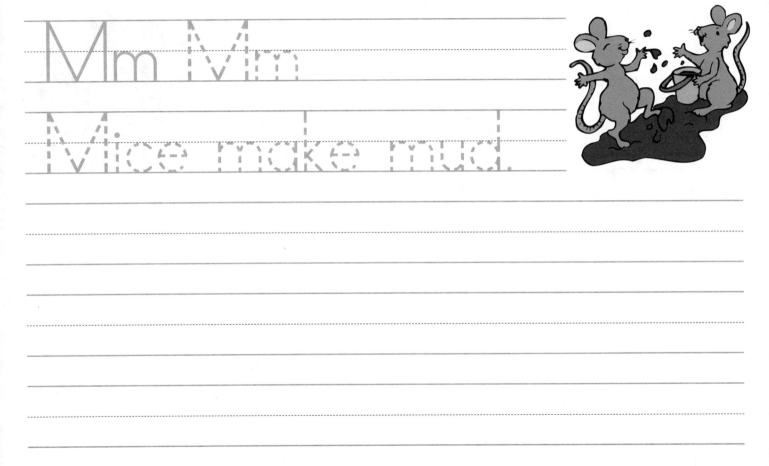

FS109029 • Beginning Manuscript Handwriting

Nn

Nn Nn

Newts nibble nuts.

Oo

O o   O o

Owls order olives.

Pp

Pp Pp

Pigs play piano.

Qq

Qq Qq

Quails quilt quietly.

46

Rr

R r R r

Rabbits run races.

Ss

Ss Ss

Seals see stars.

FS109029 • Beginning Manuscript Handwriting

Tt

Tt Tt

Tigers try treats.

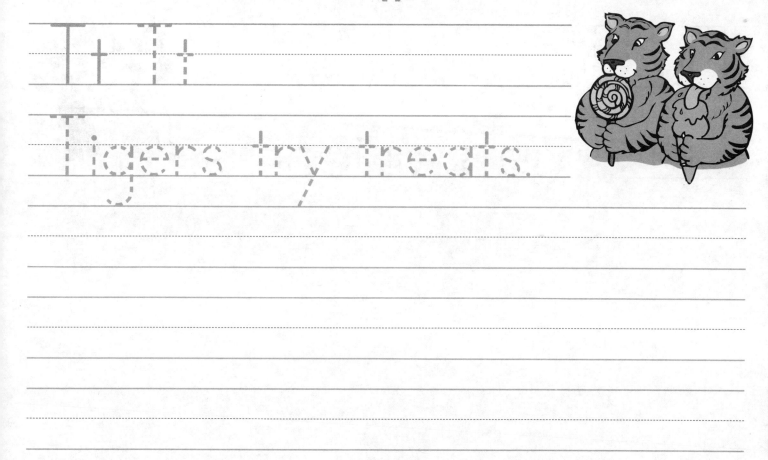

Uu

Uu Uu

Uri upsets unicorns.

FS109029 • Beginning Manuscript Handwriting

Vv

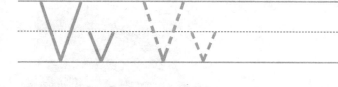

Vv v v

Vultures vacuum.

Ww

W w W w

Whales wear wigs.

FS109029 • Beginning Manuscript Handwriting

Xx

X Xx X Xx

X-rays excite Max.

X-RAY

Yy

Yy Y Y

Y

Young yaks yawn.

Zz

Zz Zz

Zebras zoom by.

FS109029 • Beginning Manuscript Handwriting

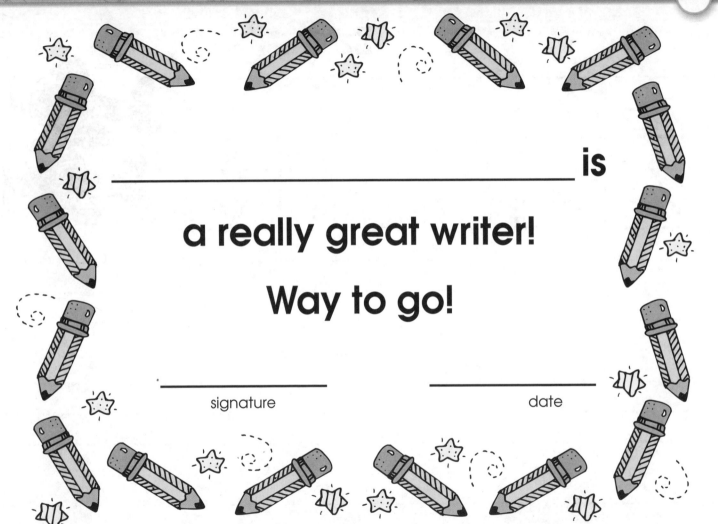

_____ **is**

a really great writer!

Way to go!

_____   _____
signature   date

FS109029 • Beginning Manuscript Handwriting